# MORGAN

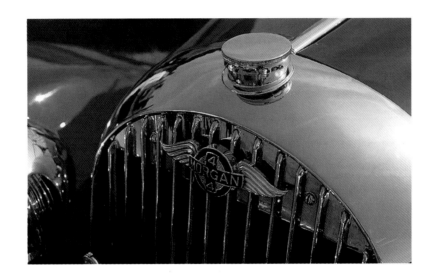

# MORGAN

Rowan Isaac

# Acknowledgements

First published in Great Britain in 1994
by Osprey, an imprint of Reed Consumer
Books Limited, Michelin House,
81 Fulham Road, London SW3 6RB and
Auckland, Melbourne, Singapore and Toronto.

© Reed International Books 1994

ISBN 1 85532 465 2

Project Editor Shaun Barrington
Editor Simon McAuslane
Page design Paul Kime/Ward Peacock
Partnership

Printed and bound in Hong Kong
Produced by Mandarin Offset

**Half title page**

*The first production four wheeler
appeared in early 1936, the 4/4 - four
wheels and four cylinders*

**Title page**

*The Grand Prix model (1913) was the
first three wheeler to have its engine
exposed to the elements*

I would like to thank the following owners and companies for their tremendous help and co-operation during the preparation of this Osprey Classic Marque volume: John Kenward, Harry Cartwright, Kelvin Lee, Chris Osborne-Jones, Dick Dumbleton, Chas Reynolds, Stuart Harper, Dave Pittuck, Maurice Williams, Derek Frampton, Tony Clarke, Bill Tuer, Gregg Bibby, Michael Bull, David Rushton, Jeremy Harrison, George Bucko, Roger and Celia Pollington, John Smith, Mary Lindsay, Michael Morris, Barney Gowar, Bob Harper, Don and Cecily Jellyman, Malcolm Adams, Alan Cameron, Charles Sampson, David Haith, Keith Robinson, Martin Stendall, Andrew King, David Giles, Terry Day, Richard Coley, Ray Salisbury, Matthew Wurr, Colin Musgrove, Roger Orford, Dick Green, Stan Thorpe, Chris Booth, Rick Bourne, Simon and Glen at E.T. Photographic (Rotherhithe, London), Central Motor Auctions (London Colney, St Albans) and Tim Bampton at Brands Hatch Circuits Ltd.

I would also like to thank Walter McGregor, Andy Abraham, Freddie Frot, Graeme Turner, Peter Sargeant, John Worral, Chris Drinkwater, John Hoar, David Rymer, Pat Kennet, John Macdonald and Rob Wells at Libra Motive for their help and generally pointing me in the right direction.

Particular thanks are due to Charles Morgan for his co-operation and for allowing me a free run of the factory and also to the craftsmen and women of the Morgan Motor Company who appear in the factory photographs.

Finally many thanks to Mike Taylor for his invaluable help, to Phillipa Crammond and her Apple Mac and also special thanks to Chris Booth, Mike Coram at F.H Douglass Ltd and Rick Bourne for checking the factual accuracy of the text.

In a mainly photographic book it has been impossible to include as much information as I would have liked. I can therefore highly recommend the following books for your further reading pleasure:

Morgan: First and Last of the Real Sports Cars by Gregory Houston Bowden (Haynes)

Morgan: The Cars and the Factory by John Tipler (Crowood)

Original Morgan 4/4, Plus 4 and Plus 8 by John Worral and Liz Turner (Bay View Books)

The Morgan Three Wheeler Gold Portfolio 1910-1952 compiled by R.M Clarke (Brooklands Books)

For a catalogue of all books published by Osprey Automotive
please write to:

**The Marketing Department, Reed Consumer Books,
1st Floor, Michelin House, 81 Fulham Road, London SW3 6RB**

# Introduction

*Morgans have been involved in motorsport from the earliest days. Most serious racers tend to replace the standard windscreen with an aeroscreen to improve the car's aerodynamics*

The Morgan Motor Company is a unique part of Britain's colourful motoring history: it is the world's oldest privately owned car manufacturer being run today by Peter and Charles Morgan, son and grandson of the founder, H.F.S. Morgan.

From the very first three wheelers of 1910 through to the current crop of four wheelers the accent has always been very firmly on open-top motoring with a sporting flavour. Indeed the company's reputation over the years has been built to a great extent on its formidable sporting achievements.

Morgan have also benefitted from three generations of shrewd business management and though its fortunes have fluctuated through two world wars, numerous depressions, various energy crises and one attack from Sir John Harvey-Jones, it has survived and seen off many of its competitors.

A visit to the Morgan factory today is like stepping back in time. Craftsmen still fashion parts by hand. Yet, despite their traditional styling, Morgan products must conform to the same swingeing safety, emission and type-approval legislation imposed on the industry's big league players. Such legislation demands a constant honing and fine-tuning programme to keep in step.

A Morgan, be it of one of the many classic models or the very latest Plus 8, is really about individualism, character and sheer driving pleasure though it was probably best summed up in the May 1930 edition of *The Cyclecar* by a reviewer who wrote: 'There is and always has been something altogether delightful about a Morgan which defies definition.'

# Contents

**Above**
*The controls and instruments of a three wheeler can appear daunting to the uninitiated. The machine-turned aluminium dashboard on this 1928 Aero model was a standard feature, as was the St. Christopher plaque bearing the chassis number*

**Left**
*Speed trials and hill climbing can be a relatively inexpensive way of getting into motorsport. Here at the 1993 Bugatti Owners Club meet at Prescott in Gloucestershire Martyn Culling puts his Morgan 4/4 to the test*

# THE EARLY YEARS

Harry Morgan, or H.F.S. as he became more commonly known, was born in Herefordshire in 1881. He was educated at Marlborough College and Crystal Palace Engineering College, going on to serve a seven year apprenticeship under the Chief Engineer at the Great Western Railway works in Swindon.

After seven years at Swindon, having graduated as a draughtsman, H.F.S. went back to Herefordshire and opened a garage in Malvern Link, initially running a local bus service and later with a partner setting up a car hire business.

Putting his design and engineering skills to effective use, H.F.S. began building his own three-wheel car, or cyclecar around 1908. The project benefitted considerably from the invaluable help provided by the Engineering Master of Malvern College, the father of one of H.F.S.'s friends, who arranged that much of the essential machining work be undertaken in the college workshops. With these facilities made available the car was complete and ready for trials by early 1909.

Of simple design and light construction the chassis consisted principally of a sturdy tube which ran the full length of the car. At the front this split into four diametrically opposed tubes which supported two transversely mounted cross members, on the ends of which were fitted the independent suspension of H.F.S.'s own design. This was a first for a British car. The only car in the world with anything comparable at the time was the French Sizaire-Naudin. Other ingenious touches were two additional chassis members which acted as exhaust pipes that connected to silencer boxes at the front of the engine.

Ahead of the suspension line was mounted a Peugeot vee-twin motorcycle engine. Contained within the central chassis tube was the propshaft, which connected to the engine through a simple cone clutch while at the rear, drive was transmitted to a single wheel through a bevel box with two dog clutches and two chains, one for each of the two speeds. There was no reverse.

The single rear wheel was mounted on two trailing fork arms supported on either side of the hub by multi-leaf quarter elliptic springs. Braking comprised of two bands on either side of the rear wheel; one

*This 1912 Sporting Runabout, owned by Kelvin Lee, is one of the oldest surviving Morgans and was discovered in the early fifties being used as a coal scuttle in a blacksmiths in Yorkshire. Despite restoration work over the years, the most recent rebuild being carried out in 1982 by Morgan specialists Roger Orford and Laurie Weekes, the car is still very original*

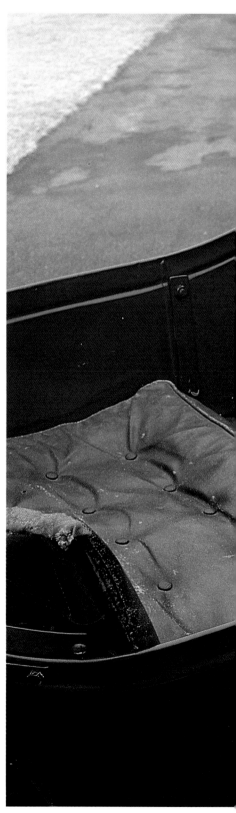

linked to the foot brake, the other applied by a handbrake. Steering was controlled by a handily located tiller mounted on the right hand side of the chassis. A single seat was fixed just forward of the rear wheel, above the bevel box. The bodywork was spartan in the extreme with a mudguard over the rear wheel only, while the petrol tank was fitted above and behind the air-cooled engine. All very simple but also very effective.

Friends and colleagues of H.F.S. were very impressed with the finished car. So much so that he was encouraged into setting up a business to put the design into manufacture. Financial support for the venture came from

**Right**

*The two seat interior is certainly spartan by modern standards but must have seemed almost luxurious at the time, especially to the many motorcyclists who, impressed by the Morgans' sporting characteristics and motorcycle-like similarities, made the move from two wheels to three. Acetylene light sets and front windscreens were optional. Dynamo-driven electric lighting came in as an option in 1914*

**Above**

*J.A.P. engines were associated with Morgan right from the start. The 1910 Olympia Motorcycle show cars featured 4-h.p. single cylinder and and 8-h.p. vee-twins. This 1912 Runabout has the 8-h.p. air cooled 964 cc vee-twin under a traditional bonnet. High and low gear ratios were 4.1:1 and 8:1 respectively. H.F.S. Morgan's patented sliding pillar and coil spring suspension can clearly be seen from the front*

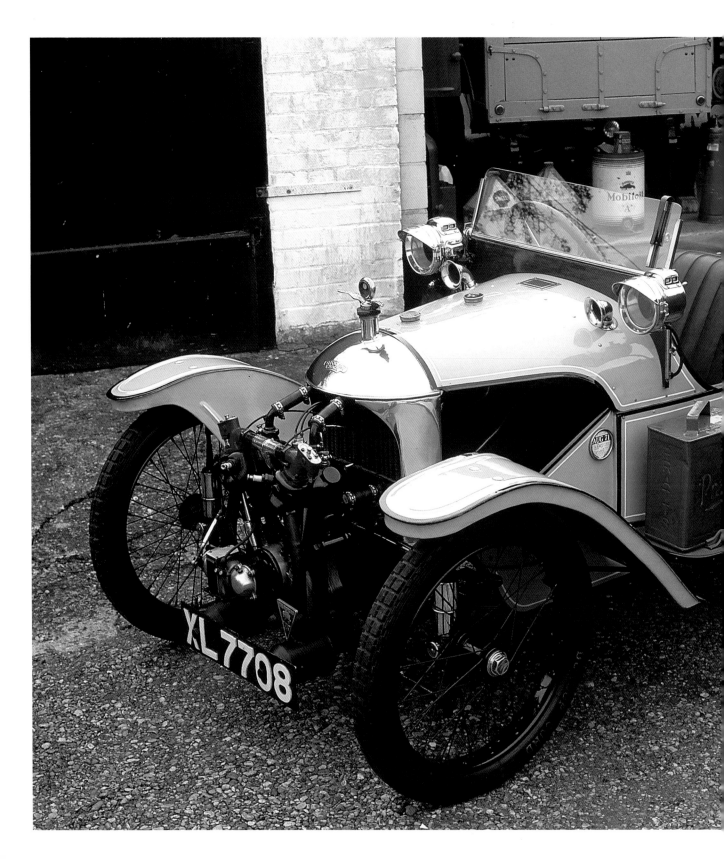

his father, Rev. George Morgan, and the Morgan Motor Company came into being.

The car had its first public outing at the International Cycle and Motor Cycle Show at London's Olympia in 1910. However, interest was only limited and sales were slow, largely because of the Morgan's single seat accommodation and unproven performance in trials and competitions.

However, these shortfalls were soon remedied. A two seater Runabout was displayed at the Motor Cycle Show in 1911, while, to gain its spurs, H.F.S. himself entered the Motor Cycle Club London to Exeter Trial, winning a gold medal. Also, an up and coming London department store by the name of Harrods spotted the Morgan's potential and became their first agent.

The two seater Runabout immediately appealed to a wide market. It was relatively practical and comfortable, featuring a hood as well as a hand starter operated from the driver's seat. Yet with its high power/weight ratio of 90 b.h.p./ton, giving the Morgan Runabout a maximum speed of 45 mph, it could be called a sportscar. Better still, at around £70 the price was within the range of many people's pockets. Moreover, its cyclecar design placed it in the same road tax category as the motorcycle.

By 1912 the Morgan Motor Company had increased in size dramatically and indeed would continue to prosper through the Great War (1914-18), when much of the firm's output was turned over to munitions production.

With hostilities over, demand for cars in the early 1920s rose significantly. Production at the little Malvern Link factory increased to 2,500 units per year, the decade proving to be the golden era for the three wheeler.

During this period Morgan used many vee-twin motorcycle engines supplied by various manufacturers such as M.A.G., British Anzani and Blackburne (Matchless vee-twins and the Ford four cylinder unit were not to be used until the 1930s). Depending on availability these engines were either fitted as standard or as an option. However, Morgan established a special relationship with J.A. Prestwich & Co Ltd, who became their principal supplier right up to the early 1930s.

*The Grand Prix model was introduced following W.G. McMinnies' win in the French cyclecar Grand Prix of 1913 and was available right up to 1926. It was the first Morgan to have its engine exposed to the elements; a look that has since come to typify Morgan three-wheelers. This 1922 example is owned by Chris Booth and is one of a number of Morgans on view in his historic vehicle collection*

**Left**

The brass work on Chris Booth's car is non-standard. Cars leaving the factory would have had nickel-plated fixtures and fittings until the introduction of chromium-plating in the early thirties. The throttle and air levers can easily be seen on the steering wheel and hidden behind the wheel on the right hand side of the dash is the ignition advance and retard lever. Starting an early Morgan was not simply a matter of turning a key; a careful '10 point plan' had to be followed: 1) Turn petrol tap on (located behind engine). 2) Flood carburettor by depressing device on float chamber. 3) Close air lever. 4) Open throttle lever slightly. 5) Half advance ignition lever. 6) Turn on oil drip feed (located to the left of the steering wheel). 7) Insert starting handle in bevel box just forward of the rear wheel. 8) Check gear is in neutral. 9) Hold valve lifter lever open (located on the body work of the car where the driver's door would be). 10) Wind starting handle and hope for the best

**Above**

In 1922 the Grand Prix model cost £160 new, with either a water-cooled J.A.P. or Blackburne engine. The M.A.G. (Motasacoche a Geneve) water-cooled 1100 cc. vee-twin, seen above, was also available for an extra £7. Carburettors would be standard motorcycle types such as Brown and Barlow, Amac or Binks

Morgan's 1924 5-car model line-up was comprehensive for such a small company ranging from the basic Popular with its 976 cc air cooled engine priced at £110, to the 1098 cc s/v Aero model costing £148. A single seater racing version was also available with a £160 price tag.

Competition in the three-wheeler market place during this period was keen, Morgan's major opposition coming from companies such as Castle Three, New Hudson, LSD, Economic and Scott-Sociable. However, within just a few short years sales of the austere three-wheeler cars were to plummet alarmingly marking the increasing popularity in small four wheel saloons, such as the Austin 7, with their four cylinder water cooled engines and practical, enclosed cabins.

From the earliest days H.F.S. Morgan took a strong interest promoting his products through motor sport entering many events himself. As early as 1912 H.F.S. had broken the cyclecar record at Brooklands, covering 59 miles, 1,120 yards in 60 minutes. 'Nearly 60 miles in one hour' the front cover of *The Cyclecar* proclaimed, a headline which generated valuable publicity for Morgan. Like other manufacturers H.F.S. understood the fundamental importance of demonstrating the strength and reliability of his products under rigorous competition conditions, good press often persuading the 'floating' purchaser of a car's merits.

With the advent of the 1930s, the motoring climate in Britain was changing dramatically. The Great Depression, which had started in the latter years of the previous decade, was putting many respected firms, such as Invicta and Swift, out of business. Even Bentley was taken over – by Rolls Royce.

For Morgan, in addition to battling against the effects of the Depression there was now competition from BSA, the motorcycle manufacturer, who launched their own three wheeler in 1929. It was a gallant attempt to challenge Morgan's position in the market place and would continue unabated until 1936, when BSA too ceased three wheeler production.

The early 1930s saw a number of significant changes to the Morgan. A three speed and reverse gearbox was introduced in 1931, and easily removable Dunlop Magna front wheels the year after. Also in 1932, the cone-type clutch was replaced by a single dry plate version. Matchless engines were fitted to the Sports Family model in 1933 and from 1934 onwards became the only vee-twin motorcycle engine available.

That Morgan survived the Depression years was due largely to

*Putting up the hood on a 1922 De Luxe model is a relatively simple operation; just make sure you're actually in the car before you start! The handbrake controlling the rear wheel band brakes was located on the outside of the car just forward of the bevel box starting handle aperture. Front wheel brakes were announced in March 1923*

careful, shrewd management; scaling down production and reducing prices until the market began gaining more confidence towards the middle of the decade. It was this same management style which instigated Morgan's most important development programme to date, which would culminate in the introduction of the first Morgan four wheeler in late 1935.

The first step in this programme was the launch of the F-type three wheeler in 1933, which featured a perimeter frame chassis of much enhanced torsional rigidity fabricated from Z-section sheet steel. This was needed to support the new Ford 8-hp four cylinder s/v engine which

**Right**
*The star attraction on the Morgan stand at the 1922 Olympia Motorcycle show was the new Aero model. Like the Grand Prix, the Aero catered for the Morgan driver with sporting aspirations. The show car featured an 8-h.p. o.h.v. water-cooled Anzani engine with Binks 2-jet carburettor, M.L. Magneto, K.L.G. plugs and exhaust-heated induction pipe. The bodywork was of polished aluminium. This 1928 example was bought a few years ago as an abandoned restoration project and has been brought back to life by owner Derek Frampton*

**Above**
*The radiator mascot was a Morgan accessory. Opinions vary on the lineage of the winged creature – some plump for stork, others are in the Pterodactyl camp. On top of the bonnet are the petrol and oil filler caps*

**Above**

The engine on Derek Frampton's Aero is a 1100 cc o.h.v. water-cooled J.A.P. and was known as the 'dog-eared' J.A.P., the 'dog's ears' being the castings carrying the valve rockers. The 10-h.p. gave 75 mph performance in high gear

**Left**

Standard dashboard equipment included a Lucas electric control panel with magneto and lighting switches and an oil sight-feed. The ignition advance and retard lever, on the dash up to 1924, was now on the steering wheel. The speedometer was optional. The St. Christopher plaque on the left of the oil sight-feed would have been factory-fitted and is stamped with the chassis number

was conveniently located behind the front wheels. Sales of the Matchless vee-twins and the new four cylinder models were initially good but, from the middle of the decade to the advent of the Second World War, it was downhill all the way for the three wheeler and in 1939 only 29 models were sold. Morgan's salvation was the introduction of the four wheeler, vindicating H.F.S.'s vision of the company's next generation of cars.

With the war over, the F-type remained in production selling in small quantities until February 1952 when the last car left the factory marking the end of an era.

**Above**
*Stan Thorpe's Aero has the optional Anzani 1076 cc o.h.v. water-cooled engine. Anzani engines were listed in the Morgan catalogues from 1923 to 1929 but were not that popular as early ones suffered from a cam profile problem which often resulted in valve heads breaking off*

**Above**

The standard Aero dashboard was of machine-turned aluminium, as on Derek Frampton's car previously. However some owners have since opted for an attractive wood version. The oil sight-feed controls the engine lubrication. Every five miles or so the pump next to the sight-feed has to be depressed in order to push oil through the engine. The oil enters the timing chest, via copper piping, overspilling into the crankcase, lubricating the big-end main bearings and the pistons. With no sump to reclaim the used oil this is known as a total loss lubrication system.

**Left**

There were no doors on the Aero model, so the Morgan treadplate on the passenger side enabled those of a less gymnastic disposition to make a two stage ascent into the cockpit

A prototype four-seater was built at the factory in 1912 but it wasn't until 1919 that they were first listed in the catalogues. The four seaters made the joys of Morgan motoring available to the family man and unsurprisingly enough they became known as the Family models. This 1925 example, fitted with a s.v. water-cooled Blackburne engine, would have cost £133 new which compared favourably with the four wheeled competition, such as the Austin 7 at £155. Colours available were grey, red, blue, purple or green; special colours being £2 extra. A six volt electrical system was now standard, with a dynamo driven from a pulley on the back of the flywheel. After 1927 the dynamo was driven from the countershaft in the bevel box

**Right**

The W.G. McMinnies win in the Amiens Cyclecar Grand Prix, as well as prompting the introduction of the Grand Prix model, also impressed the French enough to seek a licence to build their own Morgan. In 1919 an agreement was reached with the French Morgan agents Darmont and Baudelocque. Though retaining the basic Morgan ideas, the Darmont-Morgan soon evolved its own body styles, as seen here in this 1925 Sports two seater owned by Dave Pittuck. Production ceased in 1939

**Above**

Darmont produced their own 'copy' versions of various vee-twin engines. Seen here is their 980 cc s/v. air-cooled J.A.P. On the crankcase the names Darmont and Morgan appear in raised lettering – the only three wheeler engines to ever appear with the Morgan name

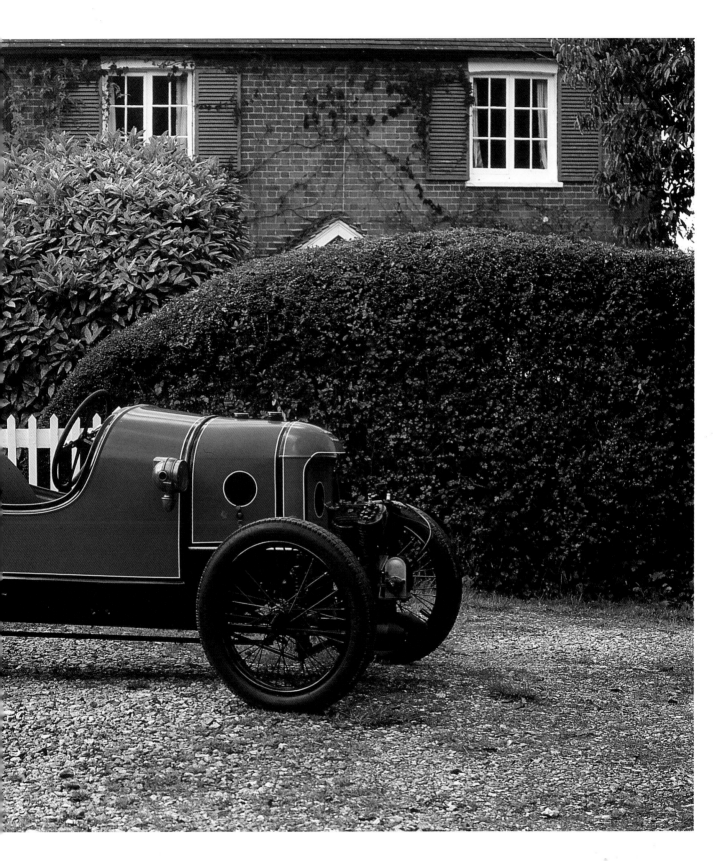

**Right**

Late 1927 saw the introduction of the Super Sports Aero model. With a chassis three inches wider and two and a half inches lower than previous Aeros the Super Sports, as it became known, was the most streamlined looking production Morgan to date. Equipped with the latest 10-40-h.p. J.A.P. vee-twin it had a top speed of 80 mph. The 'beetle-back' rear end was hinged to allow access to the rear wheel and the battery. Owners of Super Sports models, such as Tony Clarke, seen here in his 1933 version, can easily be recognised by the holes burnt in the elbows of their clothing

**Above**

The radiator mascot with built-in temperature gauge is a period accessory

**Left**
Tony Clarke bought his *Super Sports* in the late Fifties for £20 but family commitments at that time meant that the badly needed restoration work didn't get started straight away. Consequently it is only in the last two years that the car has been on the road. The 1096 cc J.A.P. vee-twin has a dry sump lubrication system. With the oil now being circulated around the engine by a pump, the dashboard-mounted hand-pump was no longer necessary

**Above**
Various contrasting chassis and body colour schemes were offered by the factory, as seen here in this 1934 *Sports* two seater. This car also has the easily removable Dunlop Magna wheels, introduced in 1932

**Overleaf**
The 'barrel-backed' *Super Sports* replaced the 'beetle-backed' model in 1934 though there was an inevitable overlap period. The barrel back solved the problem of where to put the spare wheel; on the previous model it was perched precariously on top of the tail. The new model was a practical as well as an attractive solution

**Left**

*Apart from still having the throttle, air and ignition levers on the steering wheel, the dashboard had by now become much more car-like. Under the skin, things had also come on a pace with the old two speed bevel box being replaced by a three speed and reverse gearbox in 1931. All round drum brakes were operated by Bowden cables; the rear braking being controlled by a foot pedal and the front braking being controlled by a centrally mounted handbrake*

**Above**

*Morgan customers had been introduced to the Matchless engine with the 1933 Sports two seater which featured a 990 cc s.v. water-cooled vee-twin known as the MX. John Kenward's Super Sports seen here has the MX2, a 990 cc o.h.v. air-cooled version. All Matchless engines were of the 'square' type in that the bore and stroke were both 85.5mm*

The Super Sports and Sports models of 1937 had the option of o.h.v. water-cooled (MX4 – as seen here on Maurice Williams' Super Sports) or air-cooled Matchless engines. The Sports was also still available in s.v. form. The long relationship with J.A.P. engines had come to an end in 1933, partly as a result of Morgan's reduced demand for vee-twins

The Family models were produced right up to 1936, overlapping with the four seater, four cylinder F-type which was introduced in November 1933. Compared with the racier Aeros, Grand Prix and Super Sports, the Family models were very much more upright and utilitarian. This restored 1935 example has the Matchless MX vee-twin under the bonnet and, being a side-valve engined family model, the exhaust system is still as per H.F.S. Morgan's original design, with the two longitudinal chassis members either side of the propeller shaft acting as exhaust pipes. Standard 1935 equipment included a horn and screen wiper being run off the Lucas six volt electrical system. The Matchless engine produced 28 b.h.p. at 3,500 rpm which gave a top speed of 60 mph and petrol consumption of 44 m.p.g. Price on the road, including the £4 Tax, was just under £100. Of the few three wheelers left at that time the J.M.B. Gazelle came in lower at £75, while the B.S.A. and the Coventry-Victor were both around the £125 mark

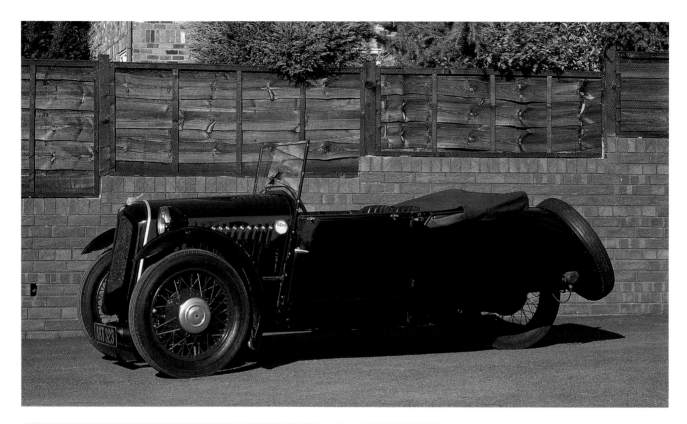

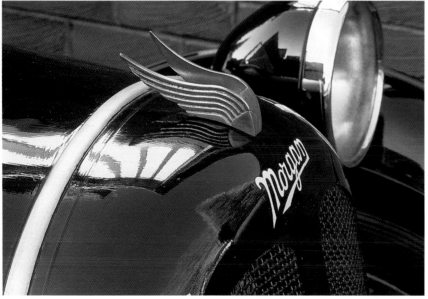

**Above**
This 1934 Family is owned by Harry Cartwright and was restored in the mid-eighties in time to win 'Best in class' at the 1986 seventy-fifth anniversary national meet at Malvern

**Left**
The winged bonnet mascot was only a standard fitting on the family models

**Right**
There were many new developments with the introduction of the F-type four cylinder model in late 1933. A new front suspension system wasn't one of them!

**Right**

The F4 was still definitely a three-wheeler but the two major changes were the more conventional car-type chassis and of course the Ford 8-h.p. four cylinder engine. The 1934 Morgan catalogues offered five different body styles; the new F4, the Family, Sports Family, Sports two seater and Super Sports. Prices ranged from £105 to £135. This particular car, with chassis number F38, was dispatched from the factory to Edinburgh in October 1934. The two-tone colour scheme is an original one, being the same as one of the Olympia show cars of that year. The car is currently owned by Chris Osborne-Jones and is used on a daily basis

**Above**

With coil ignition and electric starting, the ignition levers on the steering wheel were no longer necessary. The central propeller shaft was still in place, transmitting the drive to the rear wheel by the usual three speed gearbox. The footbrake now operated on all three wheels with the handbrake as a parking brake on the rear wheel. The clothes peg is not a standard Morgan fitting, but can be purchased at most reputable hardware stores

**Above**
The rear body-styling was a cross between that of the Sports two-seater and the Super Sports. Access to the rear wheel was gained by removing the spare. Rear wheel removal is made easier by the provision of a knock-out spindle which enables the wheel to be detached complete with the chain sprocket

**Left**
H.F.S. Morgan had experimented with a four cylinder Dorman engine and a Coventry-Climax before deciding on the 8-h.p. s.v. Ford unit. The bore and stroke were 56.6mm and 92.5mm respectively giving 933 cc

Up to the Second World War the F-type was available in two basic body-styles, the four seater F4 and the two seater F2 (introduced in 1935 along with the optional 10-h.p. 1172 cc Ford engine). After the war a final batch of about 9 Matchless vee-twins was shipped to Australia, leaving three wheeler production restricted to the F4 and a two seater F-Super. Demand for three wheelers had been dropping from the mid thirties onwards and from 1946 to their demise in 1952, only around 250 F-types were built. This 1946 F-Super would originally have had sweeping wings connected to the bodywork as on the F4. The cyclewings are a later non-standard owner modification that mimicked the pre-war F-type Super Sports model which ran from 1937 to 1939

The Morgan Three Wheeler Club is a thriving concern providing members with technical back-up, specialist knowledge and a spares manufacturing operation as well as the more usual social activities. Events are organised at regional centres and also on a national basis with the A.G.M. being held in Malvern, naturally. Here at a Brooklands weekend organised by the separate Morgan Sports Car Club, owners get a chance to drive their cars around what is left of the famous banked circuit and to put their hill-climbing abilities to the test

*A good turn-out at a camping weekend organised by the South-East centre. Owners are quite happy to drive half way across the country to attend these meetings. There are also occasional sorties into Europe to attend international events*

**Above**
Between 1927 and 1939 Morgan produced approximately thirty van derivations, all to special order. Working to an original photograph supplied by the factory, Malcolm Bull has built his own version based on a 1932 three-speeder chassis

**Right**
A couple of young three-wheeler enthusiasts take a spin around Weston Park during the M.O.G. '93 national meeting

**Above**

Many J.A.P. and other vee-twin component parts are now being re-manufactured and can now be purchased through the club. Seen here are some component parts from a 1929 'dog-eared' J.A.P. awaiting a rebuild

**Left**

Being of relatively simple design, technology and construction, the three wheeled Morgan is not necessarily the most difficult of cars to work on. If – or rather when – you need it, specialist knowledge and expertise is readily available. Dick Green is very much an engine and gearbox man. Pictured in the foreground are the cylinder barrels of a 'dog-eared' J.A.P. On the bench is an 1100 cc o.h.v. water-cooled J.A.P., a three-speed gear box and a pair of rear suspension forks, both from Dick's own Sports Family model

**Above left**
The basic chassis design of 1910 remained largely unaltered for the duration of the vee-twins though, obviously, modifications and adjustments were made along the way. This chassis, numbered R100, was one of the first of the three-speeders introduced for 1932 and was known as the R-type; the R referring to the gearbox oil to be used – Castrol R. The subsequent D-type used Castrol D. Previous chassis from 1921 had been labelled; narrow B, wide B, M and C though these letters did not refer to any Castrol lubricant. The 'narrow' and 'wide' labels refer to the width of the bevel box and not to the track as one might assume. Being fitted with a side-valve J.A.P., the tubes either side of the central propeller shaft are playing their dual roles of chassis members and exhaust pipes, with the silencer expansion boxes protruding at the front. A side-valve engined car could be specified with a conventional exhaust at extra cost, though the majority used the chassis system. Despite its lightweight appearance the three-wheeler chassis has proved to be very robust. With no nooks, crannies or nasty Z-sections to collect dirt and water, it can easily outlive a more conventional chassis

**Left**
The early R-type chassis still had a cone clutch. The Borg and Beck single dry plate clutch didn't appear until late 1932

**Above**
The 1096 cc Blackburne vee-twin was available from 1923 to 1927 and was very popular with competition-minded Morgan enthusiasts. Newton telescopic shock absorbers were fitted as standard on Super Sports models from 1927

**Above**

When he's not tinkering about with his own Super Sports, Roger Orford specialises in bodies, doing all the woodwork and metalwork himself in his workshop a few miles west of Malvern

**Right**

A recently completed restoration project is this 1935 Family. The chassis, engine and bonnet were all salvageable but the car was generally in pretty poor shape, so a new frame and various new panels were needed. All the work, apart from the hood and interior trim was done by Roger, including the paint job which was actually done in the open air on a very calm day using modern two-pack acrylic paint. All three-wheelers and indeed some early four wheelers would originally have been hand-painted

# Three Wheeler Motor Sport

The Morgan three wheeler achieved great success in the sporting arena, showing its prowess in trials, speed tests and racing.

Trials, such as the London to Edinburgh event, consisted of timed stages contested over a variety of conditions designed to test a car's speed, reliability and efficiency to the limit. Similar to the RAC Rally of today, the Morgan contingency normally comprised of works-entered as well as privately entered machines.

In 1913 two Morgans, driven by H.F.S. himself and a Mr Blackburn, were among twelve cyclecars entered in the Lake District A.C.U. Six Day Trial. Weather conditions during the whole event were poor. On the second day the route included a five mile climb through Sedbergh and Dent over an unmade track to Ingleton and finished with a 1-in-4 hairpin bend. Many of the cyclecars found the conditions too severe and retired, although H.F.S. lasted the course finishing second only to a G.W.K. on the 6th day, gaining a gold medal and much valuable publicity.

The greatest achievement of the year, however, was W.G. McMinnies' victory in the Cyclecar Grand Prix at Amiens in July. Of 38 cyclecars entered, 4 were Morgans driven by H.F.S. Morgan, W.G. McMinnies, a Mr Holder and a Mr Mundy.

All the Morgans had been specially prepared for the event with chassis 11 inches longer than standard allowing the seats to be set lower, either side of the propshaft. Best & Lloyd semi-automatic drip feed lubrication systems were fitted with foot-controlled oil pumps. Engines had to be under 1,000 cc capacity; H.F.S. and McMinnies ran o.h.v J.A.P units while Holder preferred a Blumfield and Mundy a Green-Precision.

McMinnies' race strategy relied on steady driving and staying the

*The Bugatti Owners' Club Prescott Hill Climb meeting is well attended by various clubs including the Morgan Three Wheeler Club. Seen here is Chas Reynolds putting his Super Sports through its paces. Based on a 1933 chassis, Chas' car has a modified and lowered body with a J.A.P. vee-twin prepared by specialist motorcycle engineers Dennis and Alan Wright. The engine is made up of a 'DTZ' crankcase with a 'speedway' top end and runs on methanol*

course. Two stops were made, once to change the spark plugs, the second occasion to fit a replacement tyre tube, McMinnies and fellow passenger/mechanic Frank Thomas completing the task in just 12 minutes.

In the event, McMinnies' driving tactics proved totally successful. At the end of the 163 mile course the Morgan finished just 3 minutes ahead of a French Bedelia at an average speed of 41.9 mph. A great achievement and a superb victory for Morgan.

Another driver who began making a name for himself during this time was Morgan enthusiast E.B. Ware, head of the Experimental Department of J.A. Prestwich. With all the facilities of J.A.P. available, Ware was able to develop some highly tuned engines for racing and trials. At Brooklands during 1914 he set a number of new records in the 750 cc class, attaining a speed of 63.09 mph over the flying mile.

After the war Morgan continued to realise competition successes and in 1923 W.D. Hawkes set new records in the 1,100 cc class in his Anzani-engined Morgan and covered the flying mile at a recorded speed of 90.38 mph, a most impressive performance for the day.

However, at the peak of their achievements, an accident occurred at Brooklands during the International 200 Mile Light Car Race the following year which would have long term repercussions for Morgan. Three works Morgans took part driven by Ware, G.N. Norris and Kingston Morgan agent, Harold Beart. Mechanical troubles beset the team though during trouble-free periods the cars were lapping at a creditable 85-plus mph.

On the 33rd lap the rear wheel of Ware's Morgan appeared to wobble. Two laps later, the car suddenly swerved across the track hitting the perimeter fence. Both Ware and his mechanic, Allchin, were thrown out of the car and, though both men survived this horrific incident, Ware never raced again.

The race continued and was won by a four wheeled Salmson. The organisers, The Junior Car Club, however, acted swiftly, banning Morgans from entering in future JCC competitions.

Luckily Morgans were not exempt from entering other events and in August 1925 Harold Beart broke various records in the 1,100 cc class setting a new speed of 103.37 mph for the flying kilometre and 102.63 mph for the flying mile, the first time a Morgan had been timed at over 100 mph.

Beart's car was a specially developed racing Morgan with a very streamlined body and a 1,096 cc water cooled ohv Blackburne engine. One unsual feature was a magneto cut-out switch located on the gearstick knob which, when pressed, momentarily reduced the engine revs sufficiently to allow gear changes without slipping the clutch.

*The informal open-plan pits area gives the public a chance to study the cars close-up. The Prescott meet forms a part of the Morgan three wheel 'Thursday Club Championship' comprising various events throughout the year including sprints, hill-climbs and circuit races*

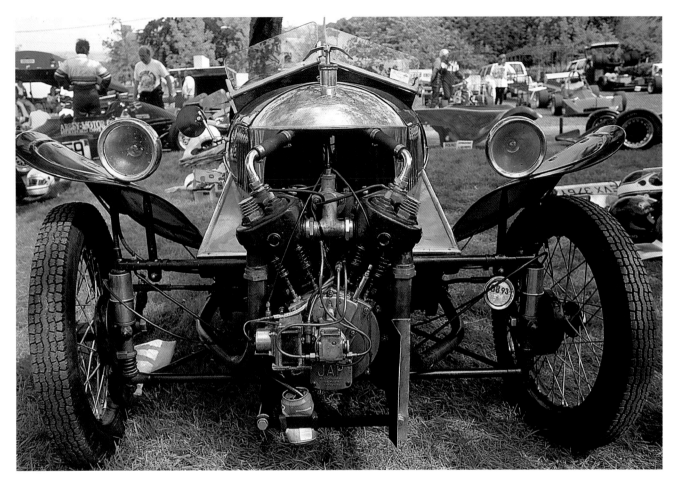

*Hill climbing can be thirsty work*

Another Morgan exponent was Gwenda Stewart, who began setting even higher speed records in the late 1920s. In 1929, driving a car prepared by Douglas Hawkes and fitted with various sized J.A.P. engines, her performances at Montlhery in France (women drivers had been banned from the Brooklands circuit since the mid '20s) were sufficient to put her name in the history books. The following year she broke even more records including clocking over 100 mph in a 750 cc J.A.P. engined car and covering 5kms at a mean speed of 113.52 mph with a similar 1,100 cc engined car, being unofficially timed at an incredible 117 mph! Reputedly the fastest female Morganist in the world at the time, Mrs Stewart's achievements did not go unnoticed!

With the newly formed Cyclecar Club, Morgans returned to Brooklands in August 1928 to enter in the club's Grand Prix event which was open to both three wheelers and four wheelers of under 1,100 cc

capacity. Contenders included Coventry Victor, Amilcar, Austin, Riley and a supercharged Salmson. The main 50 mile event of the day was won by Clive Lones in his J.A.P. engined Morgan, winning three classes simultaneously.

Morgans also competed against four wheelers in the Light Car Club Relay Grand Prix during the 1930s and, despite being heavily handicapped, a team comprising of Lones, Laird and Rhodes finished second in 1933 and '34 in special works J.A.P. engined Brooklands models.

With but a few exceptions this marked the end of the Morgan three wheeler's successes in motor sport, the baton being passed to the four wheelers to once again do battle in trials and rallies. However, on the track it would not be until the 1960s that the name of Morgan would once again reign supreme.

**Above**
*Gregg Bibby and 'riding mechanic' Ronnie Shore competing in a round of the Vintage Motorcycle Club Championship at Three Sisters circuit near Wigan, Lancashire. Morgan three wheelers have of course been associated with motorcycles right from the start. Within the VMCC they race against the motorcycle and sidecar outfits*

**Above**

Bill and Maggie Tuer and pit crew awaiting the start of their race at Three Sisters. Bill Tuer's car is very similar to Greg Bibby's, being based on a lowered and lengthened 'beetle-back' Super Sports. The 1938-type J.A.P. engines used produce about 100 b.h.p. giving a top speed on a long straight of about 120 mph. Again methanol is the preferred fuel. Bill and Greg have been racing Morgans for well over 20 years

**Right**

Bill Tuer leads the way around the twisting Three Sisters circuit followed by a Vincent Rapide sidecar outfit

**Right**
E.B. Ware, through being head of the J.A.P. experimental department, was involved with Morgans from the very early days and raced various models up until his unfortunate Brooklands accident in 1924. This 1971 replica, built by Stuart Harper, is based on a special-bodied car that Ware designed and built in the early twenties

**Above**
Being based on a pre-1930 two speeder, Stuart Harper is able to campaign the car in Vintage Sports Car Club events and has done so with great success over the last few years, winning the Dick Seaman Trophy in 1990

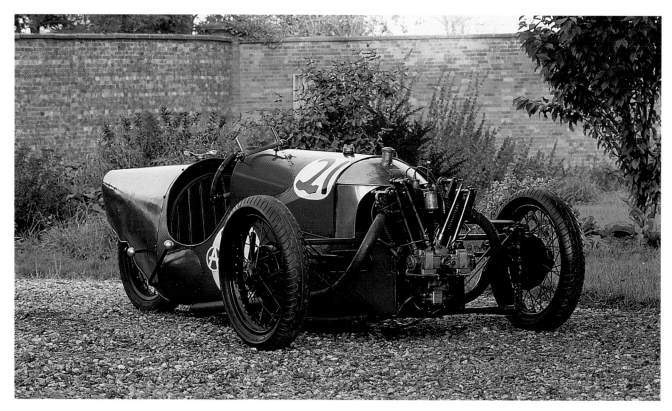

**Above**

*With its wide front track and low, rakish body styling it's easy to see how the Morgan is able to stick to the track. The engine is a J.A.P. JTOR, bored out to give 1,260 cc and develops about 90 b.h.p. A pair of Hartford friction-dampers are fitted to the rear wheel with Newton telescopic shock-absorbers at the front*

**Left**

*The lack of dials on the dashboard enables the driver to concentrate his mind on the road ahead*

**Above**

*In the 1933 Relay Grand Prix at Brooklands a Morgan team comprising of Clive Lones, Henry Laird and Tommy Rhodes achieved a creditable second place at an average speed of 89.01 mph. The winning MG team only averaged 88.62 mph but were placed first due to the handicapping. All three Morgans were special works 'Brooklands' models. The Rhodes car seen here was rescued from the proverbial scrapyard in 1955 and restored to its former glory by current owner Bill Wallbank*

**Above**

The original 1933 engine was a J.A.P. JTOR not fitted to production models. The 996 cc vee-twin had a bore and stroke of 80mm x 99mm and developed 8-55-h.p. It was race prepared by a Mr Baragwanath who specialized in tuning vee-twins when he wasn't racing Brough motorcycles. The extra tweaking allowed Rhodes to lap the bumpy Brooklands circuit at over 100 mph. This engine is currently fitted to the Clive Lones car which is also still in existence. The engine now on the Rhodes car is the same type of J.A.P. JTOR and was originally prepared by Eric Fernihough. Fernihough had prepared and raced Morgans from the mid-twenties onwards and set many class speed records with single-cylinder as well as vee-twin J.A.P.s. The red can is the 'oil-catcher', catching the oil blown out from the crankcase breather; an obligatory fitting when racing

**Right**

Though resembling a Super Sports of the day, the 'Brooklands' racer was again lower, longer and wider tracked. A hump was necessary on the beetle-back to accommodate the rear shock absorber. Bill Wallbank has regularly raced and sprinted the car over the last 35 years at home and abroad, including a couple of memorable meetings at the Nurburgring in 1979 and 1980

# A WHEEL AT EACH CORNER

By the mid 1930s the popularity of three wheel cyclecars was fading markedly. Manufacturers such as Morgan would have to respond decisively if they were to survive. It was therefore not entirely unexpected when Morgan announced their first four wheeler in 'The Light Car and Cyclecar' just two days after Christmas, 1935.

Called the 4/4 (four wheels, four cylinders) the prototype was based on the Morgan F-type chassis and powered by a Ford 993 cc S/V engine, although production models would be fitted with the more powerful and sporty 34 b.h.p. Coventry Climax 1,122 cc engine, and later still the 39 b.h.p. Standard 'Special' engine.

Body styling of the 4/4 reflected period trends with flowing wings front to rear with integral running boards, a long louvred bonnet, bench-type seating with space behind for luggage and two spare wheels mounted vertically at the rear.

H.F.S. immediately entered the 1935 London-Exeter Trial, which took place between Christmas and New Year gaining a Premier Award, thereby giving the new Morgan much valuable publicity.

By October 1936, when the 4/4 took its place on the Morgan stand at the London Motor Show, several important improvements had been made including a better cooling system, a revised dynamo and timing drive, improved steering and suspension and the addition of rubber engine mountings to reduce vibration.

Retrospectively known as the Series I, 4/4 production ran from 1936 to early 1951 with a break in manufacture during the Second World War, when only the spares and service departments remained operational, the rest of the factory once again being given over to the war effort. (Spitfire

*The 4/4 series I roadster was a very stylish car with a typical thirties 'look'. It was originally known as the 4–4 but for some unexplainable reason this changed to 4/4 after the war. Malcolm Adams's 1947 example was in a sorry state when he bought it in 1979; lots of parts were missing and what there was of the body was wrong. In recent years he has carefully brought the car back to life and has won many local and national concours events including a win in the 'flat-rad' class at MOG '92 in South Wales*

undercarriage parts were produced in the machine shop). In 1937 a four seater version was launched with a stylish drophead coupe model a year later. A total of 1315 4/4s were built.

Returning to peace time operations for most manufacturers, Morgan included, was severely hampered by the shortage of raw materials such as steel. To be assured an allocation the company had to guarantee that a proportion of their output would be exported, which in 1948 led to agencies being established in the USA and France. More international agencies were quickly set up. Indeed the '50s were to prove the halcyon days for British sports sar makers generally. Morgan themselves were exporting up to 85% of factory production to the States in the latter half of the decade.

In 1950 Morgan launched the Plus 4 (plus standing for more oomph!) as a replacement for the 4/4, available in two seat, four seat and drophead versions powered by the reliable 68 b.h.p. 2,088 cc 4-cylinder Standard Vanguard engine. Though the body styles were virtually unchanged, the new models were bigger all round and the Morgan's sliding pillar front suspension could now be pressure lubricated with engine oil.

The mid-fifties saw a number of major styling changes to the Plus 4. In 1953 the traditional 'flat rad' front was replaced by a more curvaceous nose section, the radiator grille being angled back and set in a rounded cowl. The front wings reached further forward over the wheels, the suspension arms covered by bodywork, while the headlamps were mounted in cylindrical fairings.

Peter Morgan, however, was not happy with the Plus 4's appearance and persuaded his father, H.F.S., into making further modifications, early versions becoming known as 'interim cowl' models. They lasted just eighteen months. The final solution was much more pleasing to the eye and, apart from a higher bonnet line, has remained virtually unaltered to this day.

From 1953 the Plus 4 roadster was fitted with the lusty 90-h.p. Triumph TR2 engine. Based on the Vanguard unit, but with smaller cylinder bore sleeves giving a capacity of 1991 cc this enabled the Morgan to be entered in under 2.0 litre competition classes. This was replaced by the TR3 unit in 1957 and later still the TR4 engine, by so doing Morgan always ensuring the Plus 4 gave good performance for its day.

1955 saw the welcome return of the 4/4, this time in Series II form. The decision to re-introduce this version was borne out of Morgan's desire to offer a cheap sports car, thus cementing a relationship with Ford which continues into the 1990s, latter day 4/4s using the 1600 cc CVH and 1800 cc Zeta units.

**Above**
Pre-war interiors featured dashboards with 'white on black' dials; post war this changed to 'black on cream'. The four-spoke 'Brooklands' steering wheel was standard on early cars

**Right**
Keith Robinson's 4/4 four seater has the pre-war wire mesh grille (carried over from the three wheeler F-type) and solid wheels. To his knowledge the only other similar car is in the depths of Norway. Keith knows the history of the car very well indeed as his father bought it new in 1938; subsequently five generations of Robinsons have sampled the Morgan's delights. The 'flying M' radiator mascots are quite rare and were originally seen on the three wheeler F-type. One of Keith's early memorable motoring adventures involved a trip to Spain in 1951 on an unofficial 'recce' of Spanish roads for the British Army – a good test for the Morgan's suspension system which featured, as ever, H.F.S.'s original sliding pillars with Newton telescopic shock-absorbers at the front and 40-inch elliptical springs with Andre Hartford scissor-type friction-dampers at the rear

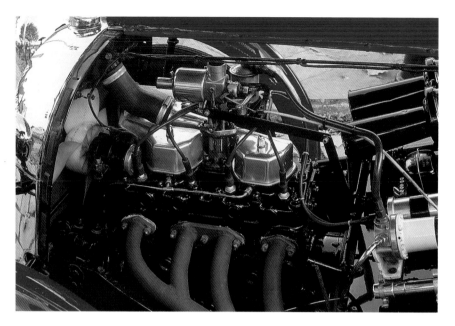

In appearance the car shared the same restyled body as the Plus 4, but with a lower bonnet line made possible by the shorter 100E s/v 1,172 cc engine. The 4/4 would continue through the Series III, IV and V forms using Ford's 105E 997 cc unit, the 109E 1,340 cc unit and lastly the 116E 1,498 cc 'Kent' unit when the series V was finally discontinued in 1968. With the exception of just one drophead coupe, and one four seater all these cars were two seater roadsters.

Morgan's huge dependency on the American market during the 1950s was to cause grave concern in Malvern when sales nosedived in 1961. (In fact, worse was to come, for stringent emission regulations stopped all Morgan sales to the US between 1968 and 1971.)

It was to be a severe lesson and consequently Peter Morgan, now in sole charge following his father's death in 1959, embarked on a major restructuring programme which involved vastly broadening Morgan's market base, establishing new agencies in Europe, Australia and Canada.

At home, the late 1950s and early 1960s saw Morgan the subject of widespread bad press, with their cars being described as out-of-date and the company too set in its ways. The buying public, it seemed, had little interest in nostalgia or craftsman-built products.

However, to demonstrate just how misguided these criticisms were Chris Lawrence won his class at Le Mans in 1962 driving a Plus 4; a commendable achievement and hailed as the beginning of a new era for Morgan on the race track. The following year Morgan unveiled the Plus 4-Plus fixed hard top coupe at the London Motor Show. A strikingly

**Right**

*The Le Mans and TT replicas were built following the pre-war successes of Miss Prudence Fawcett in the Le Mans 24hr. race and the Morgan Ulster-TT team. These cars were distinguishable from the ordinary roadster by having cycle wings at the front and a single spare at the rear; on the Le Mans this was recessed into a sloping rear panel and on the TT it was mounted on top of a solid panel. 80 mph performance was delivered by a 1098 cc Coventry Climax engine which featured a balanced crank shaft and flywheel with either a Solex or Zenith carburettor. A total of only eight Le Mans and TT models were built and consequently they are much sought after. Just to confuse matters a number of other cycle wing cars were built just before the war, possibly as a result of a shortage of steel or perhaps because it was specified by the original customer, as was maybe the case with Martyn Stendall's car seen here*

**Left**

*Martyn's car features the Le Mans spec engine and has a four branch exhaust manifold. The Coventry Climax engine has a thermo-syphon cooling system with no pump, fan or thermostat, so many owners fit an electric fan in order to cope with modern traffic conditions*

**Above**

The stylish looking 4/4 series I drophead coupe was introduced in 1938 to compete with the likes of MG, who had recently bought out their own coupe, and was based on a prototype produced for Morgan by Avon Motor Bodies. With its full height doors and fixed windscreen, the cabin has much more of a closed- in feel about it. The hood, which was fixed to the bodywork at the rear, could be folded down completely or rolled back to the halfway 'coupe de ville' position. Door handles, which were (and still are!) optional extras on other models, were standard. Semaphore pop-up trafficators were standard on coupes while left and right arms were still the norm on roadsters. The price new in 1938 was £236. This particular 1949 example is owned by Ray Salisbury and, like all post war Series I cars, has the Standard Special engine

**Above right**

The Plus 4 model was announced in The Autocar in September of 1950 and for the first three years of its life it was a 'flat-rad' available in two seater, four seater and drophead coupe form. All models initially used the standard Vanguard engine until the introduction of the TR2 in late 1953. This particular coupe, recently acquired by Richard Coley (he swopped his Plus 8 for it), left in the factory in April 1953 in lhd form and was shipped to the States. Of the 117 'flat-rad' coupes built, only 37 were for the home market. Richard's car arrived back in this country in 1988 and was converted to r.h.d.  At some stage in its life the Vanguard engine has been replaced by the later TR2 unit – hence the non-standard extra louvre panel on the bonnet

**Right**

As a result of new front-headlamp height regulations and a dissatisfaction with the styling, only 19 'interim-cowled' Plus 4s were produced. This particular car, owned by John Smith since 1971, was the first of its type off the production line in late 1953, bearing chassis number T3000, and was despatched to what was then Rhodesia now Zimbabwe. This was the first model to have the 1991 cc TR2 engine: with a bore and stroke of 83mm x 92mm, a compression ratio of 8.5:1 and twin SU carburettors it developed 90 b.h.p. at 4,800 rpm. All this development meant that it was the first production Morgan capable of 100 mph performance

**Above**

Many Morgan owners don't know the meaning of the word 'hood' so the flying hat and goggles became essential accessories, especially in the winter. To keep the feet warm a Smiths recirculation heater or 'fug-stirrer' was introduced as an option in 1952. With hill-climbing and historic rallying in mind, Andrew King has fitted a modern roll bar to his recently restored car

**Above right**

The 'high-cowled' Plus 4 was introduced in mid-1954 and was a definite improvement on the previous 'interim-cowled' model. The graceful styling of the rear body work remained, though this changed in 1955 when one of the two spares disappeared, and again in 1958 with the adoption of a flat sloping rear panel with recessed spare. Andrew King's car bears chassis no. 2336 which actually pre-dates the 'interim-cowled' model; Research has so far proved inconclusive but it may well be that this was one of a number of flat-rad Plus 4s that went back to the factory to be rebodied after the introduction of the 'high-cowled' look

**Right**

Options introduced in 1954 included a rev counter, seen to the right of the steering-wheel and flashing indicators operated by the cream switch to the right of the rev counter. The dashboard had attractive brown on cream dials up to 1962

**Left**

The Plus 4 four seater drophead coupe, or 'Snob Mog' as it became known, is a relatively rare car. Only 51 were originally built and the majority of those that are left now reside in the USA. The 1951 prototype was a 'flat-rad' version, but by the time it was offered to the public in 1954 it had adopted the 'high cowled' look. The rear end styling was somewhat different with no sign of a spare wheel; this was tucked away in the small upright boot. Production ceased in 1956. This example, owned by Terry Day, received the 'Best Plus 4' accolade at MOG '91 in Malvern

**Above**

The 29 'Snob Mogs' sold in the UK all had the 2088 cc Standard Vanguard engine. This four cylinder unit, with a bore and stroke of 85mm x 92mm and a compression ratio of 6.7:1 produced 68 b.h.p. at 4,200 rpm. This gives performance figures of 85 mph, 0-60 in 14.1 seconds and 25.6 m.p.g. 'Snob Mogs' for export all had the TR2 engine

The 4/4, in series II form, was re-introduced to the public at the 1955 Earls Court Motor Show. However, a lot of water had passed under the proverbial bridge since the demise of the 'flat-rad' series I in 1950. In the short space of five years the 4/4 had metamorphosed into the general shape that would last the next forty years (and beyond, more than likely). Presumably the styling department, having had a busy time of late, went home at the end of a day sometime in 1954 happy in the knowledge that they had done a good job, never to return! This particular car,

owned from new by Don and Cecily Jellyman, (Don actually taught himself to drive and took his test in it) is one of those Morgan anomalies, being a series II model but having a series III body. The slightly wider series III bodies were produced before the series II, with its 100E 1172 S/V engine and slightly narrower width tyres, had finished. The tell-tale sign is the extra overhang in the wheel arches. Apart from having new MOT-compulsory rear reflectors, the car is in very original condition. The rear overriders were standard, a complete bumper optional

Roger and Celia Pollington's 4/4 series IV is one of 206 built between 1961 and 1963. The series IV originally had the Ford 109E 1340 cc Classic engine producing 62 b.h.p. which was certainly a step up from the 39 b.h.p. delivered by the series III 105E 997 cc engine. However, the Pollington's car has the later series V 116E Cortina 1,498 cc unit. Series IIs used a Ford three speed gearbox while series III and IV had four speeds. On all models with the gearbox and engine being fitted as one unit, the gearchange had to be by remote linkage with the gearstick appearing from under the dashboard. Despite being in everyday use (averaging about 10,000 miles a year) the Pollington's car has had to 'perform' at shows and rallies and has won a number of 'Workhorse' concours events. The top bonnet louvres were an optional extra on the 4/4

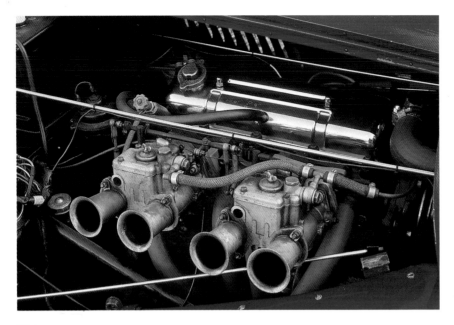

**Right**

The Plus 4 Super Sports was based on Chris Laurence's highly-tuned competition car 'TOK 258' which he raced in the late fifties and early sixties culminating in his Le Mans win in 1962. Early models (the first was delivered in March 1961) had the standard Plus 4, 'high-line' cowled body, but in 1963 the 'low-line' 4/4 cowled front end was adopted. The only immediately recognisable feature denoting the Super Sports was the bonnet scoop that allowed for the side-mounted Weber carburettors. The TR engines were specially prepared by Chris Lawrence at his west London workshops and then sent back to Malvern to be fitted with their Plus 4 chassis. The cars were then clad in lightweight aluminium except for the scuttle and cowl which were steel. The total weight of the finished car was 1,736 lb – 148 lb lighter than the standard Plus 4. There were just over 100 Plus 4 Super Sports built of which only two were four seaters. The four seater seen here was built originally for Cranfield Morgan agent, Eric White, but is presently owned by Alan Cameron who regularly competes with it in the Morgan Challenge race series. The whereabouts of the second four seater is a mystery – a 'holy grail' for somebody perhaps?

**Above**

Having arrived at Chris Lawrence's workshop the TR3/3A/4/4A engines were completely stripped down with the clutch, flywheel, con rods and crankshaft being sent to Jack Brabham Motors for balancing. Other refinements included a polished and gas-flowed cylinder-head with a compression ratio of 9:1 and a high lift camshaft. Carburettors were either 42 or 45 DC OE Webers. With the lower bonnet line models a separate header tank was fitted to the bulkhead, necessitated by the radiator having been cut shorter. An oil-cooler was also fitted forward of, and slightly below, the radiator. With the TR3 engine the Super Sports delivered 115 b.h.p. at 5,500 rpm giving it a top speed of 122 mph and 0-60 in 7.6 seconds

handsome car it showed the doom peddlars that Morgan could, after all, move with the times.

Based on the Plus 4 chassis the Plus 4 Plus utilised an all fibre glass body. Only the traditional Morganesque grille gave any hint to the car's origins. Full-width body styling with a wing-line carried through from front to rear produced a Morgan shaped like no other while the cabin, somewhat bubble-shaped, gave room for two with extra space behind the seats. There was even a conventional boot for the spare wheel and luggage. Whatever next!

The car was generally well received, though perhaps a little too radical for most Morgan buyers. And, while the Plus 4 Plus was not a financial disaster for the company sadly, only 26 were sold between 1963 and 1967.

By 1966, Triumph were about to replace the TR4 engine with a six cylinder unit designed for the TR5. Regrettably, it was too long to fit the Plus 4's engine bay. By coincidence, in May that year, Rover made friendly overtures to Peter Morgan over the possibility of a takeover and during discussions, Rover's new (and still secret) 3.5 litre V8 engine cropped up. Peter Morgan politely declined the takeover but knew that the engine, adapted from a Buick/Oldsmobile V8, was light and compact and would be ideal for a new Morgan, so when it was offered he accepted with alacrity.

The work of building the prototype was entrusted to Maurice Owen, an experienced racing engineer who had offered his services for just such a project to Peter Morgan. Initially unable to take delivery of a Rover V8 a modified Buick unit was substituted, squeezed into a Plus 4 chassis and linked to a Moss gearbox (used by Morgan since 1938) deemed able to take the huge increase in torque. Morgan's sliding pillar front suspension (fitted to all production Morgans from the beginning) was also considered worthy of the job, though the steering needed modification to a collapsible type, with joints to clear the wider cylinder block. At the rear, the leaf-spring anchorage points were lowered at the front and raised at the rear to negate axle trap.

After months of hard work the prototype had its first road test late one February night in 1967, locals in the Malvern hills being woken from their slumbers by a Morgan singing a very different tune.

Both Peter Morgan and Maurice Owen were delighted with the new car. However, that spring, Rover were taken over by British Leyland, which prevented Morgan from launching their V8 until after the introduction of the Rover 3500 saloon in April 1968. Fortunately, this gave time for further developments including fitting bigger petrol tanks, a more powerful brake servo and triple windscreen wipers. The car was displayed at the London Motor Show in October.

**Above right**
*The Plus 4 Plus, introduced in 1963, was an attempt by Morgan to keep up with the times – this was, after all, the swinging sixties and style and innovation were the order of the day. The glass fibre body was produced by E. B. Plastics of Stoke-on-Trent, Staffordshire, and was mated with a standard Plus 4 chassis and running gear. The attractive front-end styling retained a Morgan-type grille with ordinary Plus 4 wings badge above. The front bumper was carried over from the Plus 4 while the rear bumper was specially produced. 23 of the 26 originally made are known to be still in existence with seven residing in the UK, thirteen in the USA and Canada, and one each in Sweden and Japan. This particular car is owned by Charles Sampson, a long-time Morgan enthusiast who actually rates the Plus 4 Plus somewhere behind the 1928 'Brooklands' three wheeler that he owned way back in the early 1930s!*

**Right**
*The general styling of the car is a mix of period trends that work well, though the 'bubble-shaped' cabin can appear slightly 'odd-ball' from certain angles. Having a more streamlined lightweight body the Plus 4 Plus was capable of 110 mph. performance and did well in trials and rallies with Peter Morgan at the wheel. However customers who wanted an up-to-the-minute coupe were still very well catered for elsewhere and for the Morgan faithful it was far too much of a deviation from the norm*

**Left**

*Morgan have offered a production four seater continuously since 1938 on various models though not on the 4/4 series II to V or the Plus 8. The styling has always been the same as for the two seater versions, being built on the same chassis, though the rear bodywork is obviously altered to accommodate the extra bench seat. The rear seat sits over the back axle and fuel tank and is therefore higher than the front seats – hence the pram-shaped profile of the hood. The extra two inch bonnet height of the four seater over the two seater can be seen here on Roger Pollington's 1990 4/4 – the tell-tale sign being the extra gap between the base of the front windscreen frame and the top left-hand edge of the door. With its four separate sidescreens and over twenty individual twist fasteners, the hood is best erected before a downpour rather than during one. Wire wheels have been optional on the 4/4 from the series V onwards becoming standard in 1990. Chrome wires have been available since 1977*

**Above**

*In the seventies and eighties wood dashboards went out of fashion; the majority were vinyl-covered to match the seat trim. In more recent times fashions have changed again and a polished burr walnut dash has been available, as an option, on the 4/4 and Plus 4 since 1988 and on the Plus 8 since 1989*

**Right**

The introduction of the Plus 8 in 1968 immediately added a new diimension to Morgan. The last of the standard-tune Triumph engines, the TR4A produced 104 b.h.p.: here was a Morgan with 151 b.h.p. on tap. The motoring press greeted the car enthusiastically, some more than others, one American columnist being prompted to write: 'Aerodynamically the Plus 8 is probably little better than Worcester Cathedral, a few miles down the road from Malvern...' The styling was, of course, as per the Plus 4 though the dimensions were slightly larger all round (1" wider and 3" longer). Over the ensuing years the dimensions have increased further still, mainly as a result of increases in track and ever wider wheels. Michael Morris's 1977 Plus 8, restored to its current condition with the help of Morgan specialist (and original owner) Bob Harper, features many 'concours' touches such as a stove-enamelled chassis, sand-blasted and powder-coated components and fittings and stainless steel nuts and bolts. The original all-aluminium bodywork is finished in one of the most popular Morgan colours – Rosso red. The 14"x 6" Milrace wheels were used on the Plus 8 from 1977 to 1982. Michael's car went on to win the Best Plus 8 accolade at MOG '92

**Above**

The Rover SD1 V8 replaced the original Rover V8 in 1976. Sitting further back in the chassis than its predecessor, this unit has a compression ratio of 9.25:1 and develops 155 b.h.p. Twin SU carburettors are employed, though these were later changed to Strombergs in 1981 with the addition of an automatic choke. There is a four-branch tubular exhaust manifold on either side of the engine with twin downpipes, two silencer boxes on either side and twin exhaust pipes at the rear

**Above**

George Bucko's car, with chassis number R7011, was despatched from the factory in December 1968 and is possibly the second oldest Plus 8 presently in the UK. The unique chromed cowl, frowned on by some purists, harks back to the early chromed 'flat-rad' cowls and was added by George after he bought the car in 1972. Though still running with its original chassis, Moss box, panels and wood frame, the engine could hardly be described as standard. The 3528 cc V8 has a gas-flowed cylinder head, bigger inlet and exhaust valves, a solid lifter camshaft, steel conrods and a special crankshaft. Carburation is by four 45 DCOE side draught Webers and there is a stainless steel exhaust system. All this helps to boost the power up to an incredible 300 b.h.p. giving a 0-60 mph time of four seconds. The 15" x 5.5" wheels are the original rough-cast alloys that were used from 1968 to 1976. Having a special die-cast for the wheels was in fact one of the major initial Plus 8 development costs. George Bucko had his car sprayed 'Almond green metallic' – a colour used in the fifties by racing Aston Martins

**Above right**

The all-aluminium limited edition Plus 8 Sports Lightweight was introduced at the 1975 Motorshow. Using the new wider bodies that would go on the later five-speed models, the car is easily recognisable by its front bumper which is four inches shorter than the wings. After 1977, with the right size of chrome bumper no longer available 'off the shelf', a specially produced aluminium alloy version was fitted. Aluminium panels became available on all Morgans from 1976. Barney Gowar's car, seen here sporting a fibreglass hard-top made by Rutherford engineering, is one of nineteen sports lightweights made between 1975 and 1977

**Right**

Apart from one four seater roadster and one two seater drophead coupe, all production Plus 8s have been two seater roadsters. However Bob Harper, a Morgan restoration specialist, has in recent years built a two seater and a four seater drophead coupe. Peter and Charles Morgan showed a keen interest in both projects but, ultimately, as was the case with the factory drophead coupe, production costs would be too daunting

**Above left**

For the first few years the Plus 8 Salisbury rear axle had a ratio of 3.58:1, which gave exhilarating acceleration but unnecessarily high revs at motorway cruising speeds. This resulted in poor fuel consumption and extra engine wear. David Rushton's 1974 model incorporates the new 3.31:1 ratio axle that Salisbury introduced in late '73. Other than that, David's car is fairly non-standard to say the least. A serious rebuild was necessitated having written it off six months after purchase in 1982, so with racing, sprinting and hill-climbing on the future agenda he decided to make a few modifications. The power was uprated to 300 b.h.p. partly with the addition of the usual 'off the shelf' goodies and partly with a few of David's own ideas: by reworking the cylinder head and using American pistons he was able to produce a different combustion chamber shape. This helped to lift the compression ratio to 11:1 – about the limit one can go to with ordinary leaded fuel. Four 2" SU carburettors are employed. To help the 'underbody' aerodynamics, the front air dam, incorporating the oil cooler, extends underneath the engine. Finally, working on the assumption that all that extra power needed extra cooling, David removed a few of the radiator slats

**Left**

The standard windscreen was thrown out in favour of an aero screen and a new dashboard was hewn out of an oak panel from the top of an old wardrobe

**Above**

With all that untamed extra power, the rear axle in its normal state has a tendency to jump about a bit when put under pressure. This is usually checked to a certain extent by anti-tramp bars and panhard rods but David wasn't happy with this solution and, following discussions with Durham Morgan agent and racing veteran John Macdonald, he came up with the idea of a reversed A-frame system. This has the desired effect of stopping the lateral twisting movement of the rear axle. David successfully campaigned the car between 1983 and 1989 in various local and national club events and, other commitments permitting, hopes to return to racing in the near future

In September a second prototype was tested by *The Autocar* who recorded a 0-60 time of 6.7 seconds and a maximum speed of 124 m.p.h, making this the fastest ever Morgan, well able to compete with other sports cars of the day.

Known as the Plus 8 this latest model from Malvern was an immediate success. Production cars used a chassis increased in width and length by 2 inches, more suited to the bigger power unit and giving increased interior room. Meanwhile, in late 1969, the Plus 4 was discontinued. The company's 1970 model line comprised the Ford 1600 engined 4/4 in 2 and 4 seater form and the blistering Plus 8 available in 2 seater roadster form only.

As Morgan entered the next decade their fortunes improved. Demand for Morgans increased dramatically, signalling the beginning of the now famous waiting lists. For example in 1976, Mike Duncan, a West Midlands agent, quoted customers a 10 year order backlog with 150 entries on his books.

In 1985 the Plus 4 was re-introduced, now with the Fiat 2.0 litre twin cam engine. Three years later this was replaced by the 1,995 cc Rover M16 twin cam engine, until this too was superseded by the Rover T16 unit in 1992.

Over the years, Morgan's Plus 8 flagship has been modified and improved. The styling has, of course, remained unaltered though the width has crept up over the years from 4'9" to 5'3". Mechanically, the major change occurred in 1990 when the Rover 3500 unit was replaced by the fuel injected 3,946 cc Range Rover unit which produces a healthy 190 b.h.p. At the same time a three way catalytic converter also became available as an option giving the 'green' Morganeer improved torque at reduced revs.

*Jeremy Harrison's Plus 8 is not easily missed in a crowd. First registered in January 1990, the car is packed with factory-specified modifications. All black parts such as chassis, crossframe, scuttle, bumper brackets etc. were shot blasted and gloss powder-coated before assembly. Various parts were polished including the stainless steel exhaust system. The lilac paint, which extends to the undersides of the wings, was mixed to pattern by I.C.I. There is no underseal anywhere on the car. The wheels and bumpers were subsequently painted in 'Amethyst metallic'. The car was obviously built with concours in mind and has won many events in its short life to date, including 'Best Plus 8' at MOG '91 and overall winner at MOG '92 and MOG '93. However, that is not to say that it is purely a show car; for it is always driven to concours events and has also been sprinted and hill-climbed. In contrast to his car, Jeremy himself is very much the shy, retiring type – the matching lilac wig he was seen sporting at MOG '93 being completely out of character with his usually soberly attired image!*

**Above**

Jeremy's car has the fuel-injected Rover SD1 3,528 cc engine which became available as an option in late 1983. This has a compression ratio of 9.75:1 and power is boosted to 190 b.h.p. at 5,280 rpm. Torque generated is 220 lb/ft. at 4000 rpm. A lot of attention has been paid to detail under the bonnet with the alternator, rocker covers and plenum chamber all being highly polished. As ever in the Plus 8 engine bay, space is at a premium, the central bonnet hinge having to be cut away to allow for the plenum chamber

**Above right**

With its two petrol filler caps the Plus 8, up until 1993, has never had the raised Morgan script seen on the top right hand corner of all other sloping back models. The specially cast magnesium alloy wheels, introduced in 1982, have a much better finish than the similarly designed wheels of 1968-1976. In 1987 the rear light housings were changed from chrome to body colour

**Right**

The 'Morgans over America' badge commemorates a memorable trip, made by Jeremy and some other Morganeers, to the States in 1990 which resulted in a number of local Morgan club concours wins in places as far apart as Niagara, Washington DC and California. Morgans have a big following in the States as a result of the majority of the Malvern factory's product being imported in the fifties and early sixties. Consequently the British contingent were enthusiastically greeted wherever they went

**Right**

Featured at the 1993 Earls Court Motor Show, David Giles' Plus 8 has the Range Rover 3946 cc V8 engine, with Lucas 'Hotwire' electronic injection, which replaced the venerable Rover 3.5 litre unit in 1990. It also has the three-way catalytic converter which became a standard fitting from 1 January 1993. The compression ratio is 9.35:1 and the power delivered is as it was in 'pre-cat' form, that is to say 190 b.h.p at 4750 rpm. Torque, however, is increased to 235 lb/ft at 2,600 rpm giving the car superior performance, being capable of 0-60 in just over 5 seconds yet well able to amble along at 1,500 rpm in top gear. A mohair hood, as seen here, can be factory specified at extra cost. Each hood, be it mohair or the standard PVC, is tailored to fit the individual car. The spotlights on David's car are non-standard Cibie 'Oscar Drives' supplied and fitted by Libra Motive, the north London Morgan agency

**Above**

There is no doubt that wire wheels enhance the already classic lines of the Morgan though up until 1993 they were only available on the Plus 4 and 4/4. Taking into account the extra torque developed by the V8-engined Morgan, Motor Wheel Services designed a wheel specially for the Plus 8, consisting of 72 stainless steel spokes surrounded by a chromed rim. At 16" x 7" these are the widest wheels to date and to accommodate them the bodywork gains an exta 2" either side, making the car nearly 10" wider than the original 1968 Plus 8

**Above**

*Morgans have been built on the same site in Pickersleigh Road, Malvern Link since 1923. The first factory was situated on the Worcester Road but, with business expanding after the First World War, more space was needed and production was moved in stages to the current site. In the heyday of the three wheeler in the 1920s the factory churned out up to 48 cars per week. These days production is down to a more leisurely 10 cars per week. A Morgan is still very much hand-built on the premises though certain parts such as chassis, rear axles, front wings and, of course, engines are bought in. A car starts its life here in the chassis erecting shop. Since 1992 chassis have been supplied by A.B.T. of Ross-on-Wye to a design specified by Morgan. Rockwell Thompson were the suppliers from the late '70s to 1992. Customers have the option of epoxy powder-coated or galvanized chassis. The brake drums, seen here on the rear axle assemblies, are produced, in the machine shop, as are various other components such as stub axles, king pins, safety belt brackets and handbrake levers*

**Right**

*A new Range Rover 3.9 litre engine waits expectantly. Before fitting into the Morgan this unit undergoes some major surgery including having its water pump cut off and refitted to the side of the engine*

**Above**

*The completed running chassis is wheeled out of the chassis erecting shop and then literally 'free-wheeled' down the access road that runs the length of the factory to the woodshop, which is not next door as one might imagine, but three shops down. Here it receives its traditional wood frame. Ash has always been used and is chosen for its strength and flexibility. The supply comes mostly from Scotland. The wood is seasoned for at least a year in the factory woodshed and then taken to the sawmill next to the woodshop for cutting down into frame sections. This 4/4 already has its rear floorboards in place which will help support the fuel tank*

**Above**

In the woodshop the frame, having been soaked in a tank of Cuprisol wood preservative, is fitted to the chassis using stainless steel coachbolts. A mastic damp course is applied between wood and metal. The build ticket attached to the engine carries all the specifications for that particular car, including the owner's name, and will stay with the car on its journey through the factory

**Above right**

The sheet metal shop is very different to the mellow 'un-car-factory-like' atmosphere of the woodshop. Here the Morgan as we know it starts to take shape. These days a majority of customers opt for an aluminium bodied car, though the scuttle, cowl and valances are always steel. Power tools are rarely used, the craftsmen preferring to use traditional snips, shears, hammers, mallets and hacksaws. The cowl is literally knocked into shape by offering up the radiator grille as a template and making any necessary adjustments with the deft use of a small hammer. The front wings have been produced by Eva Brothers of Manchester since 1950. The radiator grille itself, having been sent away to be chromed, is finally fitted in the despatch bay

**Right**

Up to 1986, Morgans were sprayed in one piece which resulted in corrosion problems along the wings and main body joints. Nowadays all panels are sprayed separately and this problem has been overcome. A car can spend up to five days in the paintshop going through the various processes leading up to the final finish. The car first receives an acid wash, which removes all rust, grease and dirt, the acid being washed off with water. After sanding down, filler is applied to give a perfectly smooth finish especially around the headlight faring welds. After another sanding down the car is etch-primed prior to receiving five coats of matt primer. It then has its final dry and wet sanding before its two coats of I.C.I. 2k two-pack acrylic – in theory, in any one of 35,000 colours. Wire wheels can be sprayed body colour, though with a better finish than seen here – this is one of the paint shop's own slave wheels

### Above

In the wing shop the car is reunited with its wings and cowl and the wing beading is applied. After the wiring, lights and exhaust system have been installed the car is sent to the Trim shop to be finished off. This is very much a mixed bag of a workshop with people working on everything from seats, dash and trim to the hood, tonneau cover and front windscreen. Most cars these days are fitted with Connolly leather, though PVC is still available

### Left

Tony Monk has the enviable job of road-testing every car, though there is of course more to his job than a twice daily jaunt around the Malvern Hills. Each car is thoroughly checked over before going to the despatch bay. This Plus 8, still to be fitted with its grille, was destined for Germany

### Right

The workings of the legendary Morgan sliding pillar front suspension are plainly on view here. The stub axle, supported above by the larger top spring and below by the rebound spring, slides up and down the king pin with the aid of phosphor bronze bushes. The damper-blade, fixed to the stub-axle assembly at one end and the chassis at the other, can be seen to the left of the orange painted Gemmer steering box. The shock absorber is an Armstrong telescopic. Since 1950 it has been possible to lubricate the system by operating a foot-controlled button in the cockpit. This dribbles engine oil via pipes onto the king pins and bronze bushes. Apart from being obviously more robust, the basic design has changed little in the last 84 years

**Above**

John Smith, Moss gearbox specialist, gives the mainshaft assembly a final visual inspection before dropping it into the gear case. Moss gearboxes were used by Morgan on various models from 1938 to 1972. Repair and servicing work was originally carried out by Moss themselves, until the seventies, ex-employee, Norton Gabb took on the job. Following the sad death of Norton Gabb in the early eighties, John Smith, who was already working with axles and transmissions assumed the role. Today he uses many of Gabb's original specialist tools, including the rotating assembly bench seen here

**Above right**

Restoring a Morgan can be an expensive and time consuming hobby but the satisfaction in having 'done-it-yourself' should outweigh the disadvantages. As ever experts are on hand through the club, the Morgan agents and of course the factory.

Roger Pollington's 'flat-rad' Plus 4 needed fairly major surgery including a complete new wood frame, which he had specially made by the factory. The chassis was re-built by Naylor Restoration who own the Rubery Owen restoration rights; Rubery Owen being the Morgan chassis suppliers up to the late seventies. Roger has fitted a TR 4 engine (completely rebuilt by TR specialists, Cox and Buckles) as opposed to the original Standard Vanguard unit as he plans to do some classic rallying

**Right**

When fitting new wood, it is eminently sensible to treat it with a preservative; something that the factory surprisingly didn't do up until as late as 1984. The floorboards have nearly always been wood. Pre-1970 Plus 8s experimented with sheet steel in the footwells but this was found to be unsatisfactory due to rotting and cracking around the engine mounts. The axle and gearbox on Roger's car were overhauled by Moss expert, John Smith

**Above**

*A rare sight – Morgans with their hoods up. Stowage space in a two seater is minimal, so most people take up the luggage rack option*

**Left**

*An awe-inspiring view in the Lake District – and the landscape isn't bad either! The annual 'Morgans at Windermere' weekend is organised by the Morgan Sports Car Club 'Tormog' centre and is very popular with its mix of glorious scenic runs, social activities, informal driving tests and concours. The M.S.C.C. is completely separate to the three wheel club, catering for all four wheel enthusiasts, though of course the two clubs do occasionally meet up at national and regional level*

**Above**

The annual national rally or 'MOG' is organised by a different regional centre each year. MOG '92 took place in Margam Park in south Wales and was very well attended. There is usually a fair sprinkling of cars from abroad, with most European countries having their own national Morgan clubs. The seventy-fifth anniversary rally held in Malvern in 1986 was attended by about 1,200 cars (including 120 or so three wheelers); the largest Morgan gathering ever, which is even more remarkable when you consider that total four wheeler production at that time, since 1936, was only around the 14,000 mark

**Right**

The concours is a vital part of the MOG event. The final polishing on the day is the culmination of weeks of preparation

**Above**
*The driving skills course involves keeping a smile on your face at all times, just in case you happen to appear on the next Morgan video*

**Left**
*Judging the concours. Every part of the car is meticulously inspected*

**Above**

*Stalls selling everything you could ever possibly want for you and your Morgan abound. You can even buy a proper Morgan, with most of the country's agencies being represented*

**Left**

*With over 60 clubs and centres around the world you could easily cover up the entire grille with badges. A mere 10 badges is the qualification should you wish to join the Morgan Regalia Collectors Society*

**Right**

*Morgan motoring: one of life's pleasures*

# Four Wheel Motor Sport

The new four wheeled Morgan lost no time in building a track and trials reputation, though initially it was the trials events that were to the fore.

Following H.F.S. Morgan's successes in the London to Exeter and London to Land's End trials in late 1935 and early 1936, George Goodall, the works manager, had three consecutive class wins in the RAC rally in 1937-38 and 1939. The class was for open tourers up to 10-h.p. The '39 event was, in fact, a double success as H.F.S. and Peter Morgan jointly won their class for closed cars up to 10-h.p., driving a 4/4 drophead coupe with the hood up.

The major pre-war racing success was that of Prudence Fawcett in the 1938 Le Mans 24 hour event. Driving a privately-entered Coventry Climax-engined 4/4, she achieved a very creditable second in class and thirteenth overall.

The petrol rationing of the early post-war years put a stop to most forms of motor sport but by the early 1950s things were almost back to normal and 1951 saw the first RAC International Rally of Great Britain. This was an event comparable with the old A.C.U. Six Days Trial consisting of timed special stages including a speed test at Silverstone. Morgans were back to their old winning ways carrying off the team prize with cars driven by Peter Morgan, George Goodall and Dr W.D. Steel.

*TOK 258, the Lawrence/Shepherd-Barron 1962 Le Mans class winner, is the most famous Morgan of them all. Originally starting out in life as a 1956 Plus 4, it was later re-bodied at the factory in aluminium lower-bonnet 4/4 style in preparation for Le Mans. As well as having the usual Lawrencetune modifications available on the Production Super Sports model, it also had an aluminium hard-top, a twenty gallon fuel tank and a 2.9:1 rear-axle ratio. Although Le Mans instantly elevated TOK 258 into the 'Halls of Fame', it certainly did not become a museum piece. Lawrence continued to race it through the sixties and in the seventies it was given a new lease of life with Robin Gray at the wheel. Gray was already competing with a Lawrencetune Plus 8 and obviously jumped at the chance of a drive in TOK. Subsequently he had a very busy season in 1974 winning the Modsports Championship in the Plus 8 and coming in second in the Thoroughbred Championship with TOK. In the early eighties, in the hands of Patrick Keen, it was again campaigned in Thoroughbred racing, achieving an outright win in 1981 and class wins in '82 and '84. David Haith has been the proud owner since 1990 and hopes to get the car back on the track in the near future*

The 1950s, though, were generally unspectacular until the arrival on the scene of Chris Lawrence in 1958. That was the year that he began his Morgan racing career, entering his 1956 Plus 4 in the B.A.R.C. Freddie Dixon Trophy series competing against other marques such as Triumph TR, A.C. Ace, Austin Healey and M.G.A. His first season, though relatively successful, was just a taster of things to come and in 1959 he achieved an incredible 21 wins out of 22 races, winning the trophy by a huge margin.

In August of that year he was also part of the winning Morgan team in the Six Hour Relay race at Silverstone, beating the Triumph TR team by a mere nineteen seconds.

Lawrence's driving skills and, more notably, his ability to get the best out an engine, had not gone unnoticed at Malvern and, consequently, Peter Morgan asked him to prepare a number of TR3 engines on a regular basis to go into a new Plus 4 model – the Super Sports.

The Lawrencetune engine, as it became known, had a fully balanced clutch, crankshaft, flywheel and con rods. Other modifications included a polished gas-flowed cylinder head, a special high-lift camshaft, an oil cooler and twin Weber 42 or 45 DCOE carburettors.

This new model was added to the Morgan range in late 1960 and the last one to be produced left the factory in early 1968.

Meanwhile, back on the track, Lawrence was still on a rising curve and in 1961 he entered the 1000km race at the Nurburgring in Germany. Unfortunately he did not finish the race but did manage to set a new 2 litre lap record, reducing the previous Porsche-held record of 10 minutes 38 seconds to 10 minutes 31 seconds.

1961 also saw Lawrence's first attempt to enter the Le Mans 24 hour race but unfortunately he was barred by the scrutineers who presumed that such a quaint, old-fashioned car couldn't possibly be a current production model, at least that was the public story at the time. An alternative school of thought suggests that the works Triumph team kicked up a fuss with the organisers on hearing of the TR3 engined Morgan entry.

Not to be deterred, Lawrence was back at Le Mans in 1962, this time with the full backing of the Morgan factory and, with co-driver Richard Shepherd-Barron taking the final 3 hour stint at the wheel, the Morgan romped home winning the 2 litre GT class. The greatest Morgan achievement since the McMinnies French Cyclecar Grand Prix win of 1913.

Lawrence continued his work as a roving international ambassador for Morgan in 1963 at the Grand Prix de Spa where a team comprising of Lawrence, Bill Blydenstein and Pip Arnold finished first, second and third in the 2,000 cc-2,600 cc class. This was an impressive feat that was

*1959 Plus 4, one destined for historic racing and with a respectable record in classic rallying, before that in sprints and hill climbs; (see page 127)*

repeated a couple of weeks later at the Nurburgring.

By the late 1960s the frenetic activity of the Lawrence dominated era had calmed down and there was a lull of a number of years which coincided with the demise of the TR4 engine and the early years of the Plus 8. However things started to pick up again in the 1970s with a number of the country's Morgan agents such as John Britten, John Macdonald, Bruce Stapleton and Rob Wells featuring prominently on the racing scene.

There were also, as ever, heroic efforts by individuals such as Chris Alford (with a little bit of help from his employer, John Britten) who had 17 class wins out of 17 starts in the 1975 Prodsports Championship, driving a 4/4. A considerable achievement considering his total racing budget for the season was only £200. In the same championship John Britten himself, driving a Plus 8, came second in class to a Lotus Europa.

Prodsports racing was to prove very fruitful for Morgans over the next few years: in the 1979 season MMC 11, the first production Plus 8, gained class wins in the CAV Championship and the DB/CCC Championship, being driven by Charles Morgan and Rob Wells respectively. Another driver who was to make a name for himself in Prodsports was Steve Cole who had an overall win in the CAV championship in 1982.

Rob Wells' introduction to Morgans had been with a 1954 Plus 4 which he had bought and club-raced in the late '60s. By 1980 things had moved on somewhat. As well as running his Libra Motive race preparation business and Morgan agency he had also found time, with the help of the factory, to build himself a very special Plus 8 to run in the Modsports Championship. With a tubular space-frame chassis and the traditional Morgan front suspension being replaced by wishbones, MMC 3 took full advantage of the Modsports regulations. The one-piece fibre glass body could be completely lifted off the chassis allowing easy access to the dry sump 300 b.h.p. V8 supplied by British Leyland Special Tuning. Competing against highly modified Elans, Marcos' and Porsches, Rob won the 1982 BRSCC Modsports Championship.

Morgans were also very successful in the early 1980s in the Willhire 24 hour race at Snetterton: a single Plus 8 with a four driver crew comprising Bruce Stapleton, Bill Wykeham, Richard Down and John Spero lifted the Commander's Cup covering the greatest distance of any single-car entry in the 1980 event. The following year a Plus 8 driven by Norman Stechman, Malcolm Harrison, Mike Ridley and Francois Duret kept the trophy on the Morgan mantlepiece; in 1982 a three man crew of Rob Wells, Chris Alford and Malcolm Paul, driving MMC 11, won the trophy. The third consecutive Morgan victory in the Commander's Cup.

The first national championship for Morgans, originally administered by Rick Bourne of Brands Hatch Morgans, was in 1985. This came about following an 'after-race-meeting' chat between Rick and fellow racer Richard Casswell in 1984. Rick had lamented the lack of any Morgans-only races and was challenged by Richard into doing something about it! Since that first season the series has gone from strength to strength and is currently sponsored by the factory, being known as the Morgan Motor Company Challenge. The series is run over ten rounds at various circuits around the country and there are five different classes ranging from class A which is for fully modified Plus 8s and turbo charged Plus 4s, to Class E for standard Plus 4s, 4/4s and 'Moss box' Plus 8s.

Moving away from the track, classic and historic rallies have featured heavily on the sporting calendar in recent years and Morgans have not been backward in coming forward. In 1993 there were 2 Morgans out of 104 starters in the London to Sydney rally. Being for cars up to and including 1968, the early Plus 8 driven by Bruce Stapleton and Doug Morris just qualified and they finished a commendable 38th out of 86 finishers. The second Morgan entry was a 1953 'flat-rad' Plus 4 owned by Barry Sumner and co-driven by 66 year old grandmother Pam Durham

**Right**

*Mary Lindsay is another stalwart of the Morgan racing scene, having been involved since the early seventies. The car she has been racing since 1975 is a very early Plus 8 (chassis no. R7021) and together, over the last eighteen years, the two of them have seen quite a bit of action, especially in long distance events. They were both part of the M.S.C.C. team in the first Snetterton 24 hour race in 1980, the team (comprising of three cars and six drivers) finishing in a creditable third place. Sadly, after 1984 the 24 hour race was only open to saloon cars, but Mary, as one of the longest serving members of the M.S.C.C./Bulldog team (as they became known) still competes regularly in the Birkett 6hr relay races at Snetterton and also in the Morgan Challenge Race series*

**Above**

The annual Silverstone Bentley Drivers Club meet is one of the highlights of the Morgan Sporting calendar. The 1992 event was certainly a highlight for Matthew Wurr and '99 OK'. He won all three races entered

**Left**

Matthew takes a breather between races while his junior pit crew go to work on the car. The stick, with different notches for specific circuits, gauges the exact amount of fuel needed for ten laps of Silverstone. Within the Morgan Challenge Race series his car runs in class A which is for modified Plus 8s of unlimited capacity. The car is race-prepared by Morgan specialists Techniques of Radlett while the engine itself has recently been uprated by TWR Power of Coventry to 4.3 litres, developing 390 b.h.p. Allegedly the fastest Morgan around!

**Above right**

Brands Hatch Morgan agent Rick Bourne sets the pace at the Birkett Six Hour Relay race at Snetterton. The 1993 event had no less than forty separate teams taking part, each team comprising of between three and six cars. The different marques represented ranged from Jaguar Mk.1s, VW Beetles and Pontiac Trans-Ams to Austin 7s, E-types and Lotus Elans. Rick's ex-works Rover 1994 cc M16-engined Plus 4 had an extra busy season winning its class (standard 4/4 and Plus 4) in the Morgan Challenge series, this time driven by Barry Sumner

**Right**

*Chas Windridge, overall winner of the Morgan Challenge series in 1991 and 1992, takes to the water on a wet day at Castle Combe in his T16 'Tomcat' engined Plus 4. The 16 valve Rover unit this time is in turbocharged form*

**Above**

MOG '93 at Weston Park was the first time a sprint had been held at the same venue as the main event and was a great success. The sprint was included as a round of both the Northern Speed Championship and the Ryobi IDC Speed Championship, these championships catering for sprinting and hill-climbing Morganeers

**Right**

Father and son, Colin and Rupert Musgrove, usually have to queue behind Charles Morgan, Peter Garland and Tony Dron to get a drive in their own car, such is its popularity. Highly modified with a Getrag gearbox, a 4HA rear axle and a full Weber Marelli fuel injection and engine management racing system, the 1973 Plus 8 develops 360 b.h.p. and is geared up to 7,800 rpm. This gives it a maximum speed of approximately 160 mph, conditions permitting, and a 0-100 mph time of 8.5 seconds. In 1989 and 1990, in the hands of Peter Garland, the car vied for position of top dog in the Morgan Challenge series, just pipped at the post in both seasons by Rob Wells in his special factory/Libra Motive developed Plus 8. Rob's main 'edge' was that his car, being based on the smaller Plus 4 chassis had better 'chuckability'. However, the Musgrove car hasn't done too badly since its rebuild in 1988, winning 29 out of the 54 races entered and never finishing lower than third. Here Rupert Musgrove ambles down to the start of the sprint event held at Weston Park during MOG '93

170
Morgan Motor Company
C.M.R.-Shell
DVRS. TONY DRON
COLIN & RUPERT
MUSGROVE
BFGoodrich

(Pam, being a veteran of these events, having competed a few years earlier in the Paris to Peking rally sharing a Plus 8 with her daughter). Barry and Pam did make it to Australia but unfortunately the ultra-fine sands of the outback were just too much for the venerable Plus 4's TR engine and as a result of a few running repairs they didn't quite make the finishing line in the allotted time.

On a slightly smaller scale, the Malvern factory still regularly fields teams of cars for the M.C.C. London to Land's End, Exeter and Edinburgh trials. Just as H.F.S Morgan did all those years ago with the first three wheelers.

*'XOV 555', a 1959 Plus 4, is another Morgan with a history. It was originally owned and raced by Ray Meredith and one of it's first successes was as part of the winning Morgan team in that year's Silverstone Six Hour Relay Race. Chris Lawrence was showing what could be done with the 2,138 cc TR engine and this prompted Ray, with the help of mechanic Tommy Thomas, to make his own car more competitive. Initially standard Lawrencetune parts were added such as Weber carbs, a new manifold and a special camshaft. Further tuning included a lightened flywheel, balanced crank and con- rods and a skimmed head bringing the compression ratio up to 10.5:1. With the addition of Koni shock-absorbers all round, twin fuel pumps, a limited slip diff. and a racing clutch, the 0-60 mph time was shaved down to 6 seconds. The car was raced, sprinted and hill-climbed very successfully by Ray throughout the sixties amd won the second Morgan-only race at the Silverstone Bentley Drivers Club meet. In more recent times the car has been given a new lease of life in the hands of Rick Bourne, the Brands Hatch Morgan agent. Following an accident at Silverstone in 1984 Rick was able to completely rebuild the car and over the years, while remaining true to Ray Meredith's original specification, he has strived to improve upon it. The cam profile, for example, has been specially designed by Rick for the TR engine. Since 1990 Rick has moved away from circuit racing to concentrate on classic rallying, achieving some notable successes in 1992 with class wins in the Charringtons International Historic Rally of Great Britain and the Mitsubishi Classic Marathon. Future plans for 'XOV' including moving into historic racing*

# Production Dates

## THREE WHEELER

### Model Type

| | |
|---|---|
| Single seater 'Runabout' | 1910-1911 |
| Standard | 1911-1931 |
| Sporting | 1911-1921 |
| De Luxe | 1911-1931 |
| Grand Prix | 1913-1926 |
| Family | 1919-1936 |
| Aero | 1919-1932 |
| Super Sports Aero (beetle-back) | 1927-1934 |
| Super Sports (barrel-back) | 1934-1947 |
| Sports Family | 1932-1936 |
| Sports two seater | 1932-1937 |
| F4 | 1933-1952 |
| F2 | 1935-1939 |
| F Super Sports | 1937-1939 |
| F Super | 1946-1952 |

### Engine availability

| | |
|---|---|
| J.A.P. vee-twin | 1910-1934 |
| M.A.G. vee-twin | 1915-1924 |
| Blackburne vee-twin | 1922-1927 |
| Anzani vee-twin | 1922-1929 |
| Matchless vee-twin | 1933-1947 |
| Ford Eight four cylinder | 1933-1939 |
| Ford Ten four cylinder | 1935-1952 |

## FOUR WHEELER

| Model | Type | Engine | | |
|---|---|---|---|---|
| 4/4 | Series I | Coventry Climax | 1122 cc | 1936-1939 |
| | Series I | Standard Special | 1267 cc | 1939-1951 |
| | Series II | Ford 100 E | 1172 cc | 1955-1960 |
| | Series III | Ford 105 E | 997 cc | 1960-1961 |
| | Series IV | Ford 109 E | 1340 cc | 1961-1963 |
| | Series V | Ford 116E | 1498 cc | 1963-1968 |
| | 1600 | Ford Kent(2737E/2737GT) | 1599 cc | 1968-1971 |
| | 1600 | Ford Kent (2265E) | 1599 cc | 1971-1982 |
| | 1600 | Fiat Twin Cam | 1584 cc | 1981-1985 |
| | 1600 | Ford CVH | 1597 cc | 1982-1991 |
| | 1600 | Ford EFI | 1597 cc | 1991-1993 |
| | 1800 | Ford Zeta | 1796 cc | 1993- |
| Plus 4 | | Standard Vanguard | 2088 cc | 1950-1958 |
| | | TR2 | 1991 cc | 1953-1957 |
| | | TR3 | 1991 cc | 1955-1964 |
| | | TR4 | 2138 cc | 1961-1969 |
| | | Fiat | 1995 cc | 1985-1987 |
| | | Rover M16 | 1994 cc | 1988-1992 |
| | | Rover T16 | 1994 cc | 1992- |
| Plus 8 | | Rover V8 | 3528 cc | 1968-1976 |
| | | Rover SD1 | 3528 cc | 1976-1987 |
| | | Rover SD1 Vitesse | 3528 cc | 1983-1990 |
| | | Range Rover V8 | 3946 cc | 1990- |